T0197458

Mermaid editations

by Sheelin Bower

Balboa Press books may be ordered through booksellers or by contacting:

Balboa Press
A Division of Hay House
1663 Liberty Drive
Bloomington, IN 47403
www.balboapress.com
1 (877) 407-4847

ISBN: 978-1-4525-9850-5 (sc)
ISBN: 978-1-4525-9851-2 (e)

Library of Congress Control Number: 2014919863

Printed in the United States of America.

Balboa Press rev. date: 1/6/2015

BALBOA
PRESS
A DIVISION OF HAY HOUSE

Open your message in the bottle.

What do the Mermaids say to you?

Listen to your messages.

Seashore memories.

What are your favorite memories?

What future memories would you like to create?

Love and gratitude.

What are you thankful for today?

Pearls of wisdom.

What would you like to learn more about?

What subjects or interests do you find fascinating and wish to research?

You are a star. Rock on!

What talents do you express in your life?

What talents would you like to develop?

Bubble bliss.

Do you remember playing with bubbles?

What did you like to play with as a child?

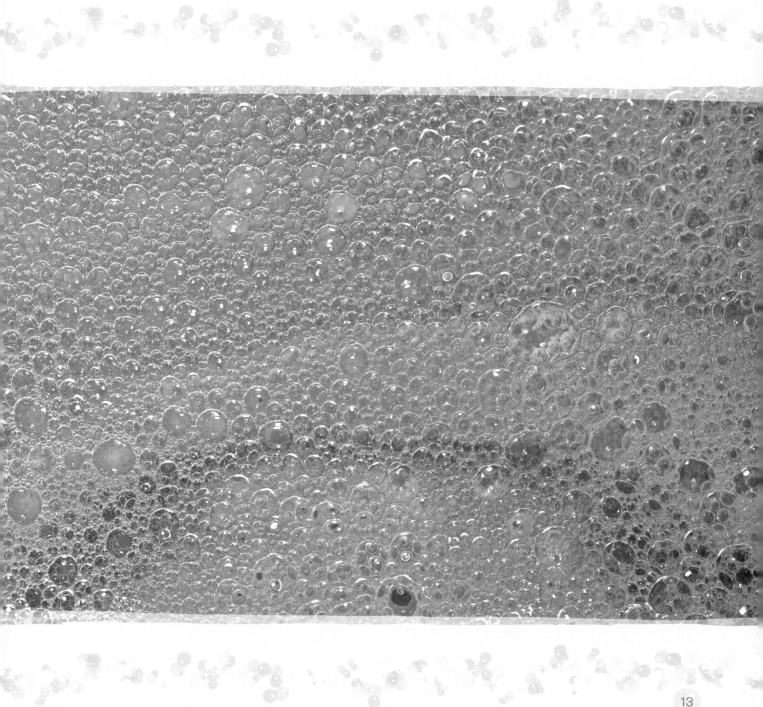

13

Happy dreams!

Enjoy your dreams at night.

Tell yourself what you would like to dream about before you go to sleep.

Keep floating.

What keeps you afloat in a temporary stormy sea of life?

Live a charmed life.

What symbols and signs do you see throughout your day?

What meanings do they have for you?

Good vibrations!

The ocean refreshes your soul and lifts your spirit.

Visit or visualize the ocean for positive energy.

Sparkle up your life.

What makes you sparkle and smile?

Let your inner spark glow!

Relax.

Cleanse your stress away.

Soak in a sea salt bath to revive your senses.

Be free!

Release the stopper and let go of bottled up feelings.

What emotions would you like to release?

27

Listen to your intuition.

What positive repetitive messages is your guidance telling you?

What are the treasures of your soul?

What gifts do you bring to the world?

What are your super mild super powers?

Abundance.

What would you like to attract into your life?

How could you go about this?

Creativity brings joy.

What are your favorite creative passions?

Accessories reflect our authentic uniqueness.

How would you like to dress and decorate yourself to express the real you?

Hi.

Practice kindness.

Being kind elevates everyone's energy.

You are so awesome!

Enhance your life with color.

What color represents you?

What colors do you like to look at?

Celebrate!

What can you celebrate right now?

What achievements, microscopic or humongous, have you accomplished?

Swim to your dreams with love.

What are your dreams for the future?

What small action step will you take to be closer to your dreams?

Plastic found on the beach.

What can you do to help keep the oceans clean and the sea creatures safe?

Thanks!

Printed in the United States
By Bookmasters